A Goat's Trick

Written by Jill Eggleton
Illustrated by John Bennett

The farmer saw the goat
looking over the fence.

"The goat is sick,"
said the farmer.
"He will have to
come inside."

The farmer put the goat
inside her house.

The goat went **munch**
on her pyjamas.

He went **munch**
on her socks.

He went **munch**
on her shirts!

The goat went
all over the house.
Munch! Munch! Munch!

The farmer looked
at the goat.
"You are not sick," she said.
"You can go out."

The goat went
under the bed.

"Come out!"
said the farmer.

But the goat stayed
under the bed.

The farmer went
to get a rope.

"I can't have a goat
under my bed,"
she said.

The farmer got
under the bed
with the rope.
No goat!

"Where are you?"
she shouted.

The farmer saw the bed
going up and down.
"Oh, no!" she said.
"The goat is in my bed!"

A Story Sequence

1

2

3

4

Guide Notes

Title: A Goat's Trick
Stage: Early (2) – Yellow

Genre: Fiction
Approach: Guided Reading
Processes: Thinking Critically, Exploring Language, Processing Information
Written and Visual Focus: Story Sequence

THINKING CRITICALLY
(sample questions)
- What do you think this story could be about?
- Focus on the title and discuss.
- How do you know the farmer was a nice person?
- Why do you think the farmer thought the goat was not really sick?
- Why do you think the goat got under the bed?
- What do you think the farmer will do with the goat?

EXPLORING LANGUAGE

Terminology
Title, cover, illustrations, author, illustrator

Vocabulary
Interest words: goat, farmer, sick, munch, rope, pyjamas
High-frequency words: her, inside
Positional words: up, down, under, over, on, out, in, inside

Print Conventions
Capital letter for sentence beginnings, full stops, commas, quotation marks, exclamation marks, question mark